The Cologne Cathedral

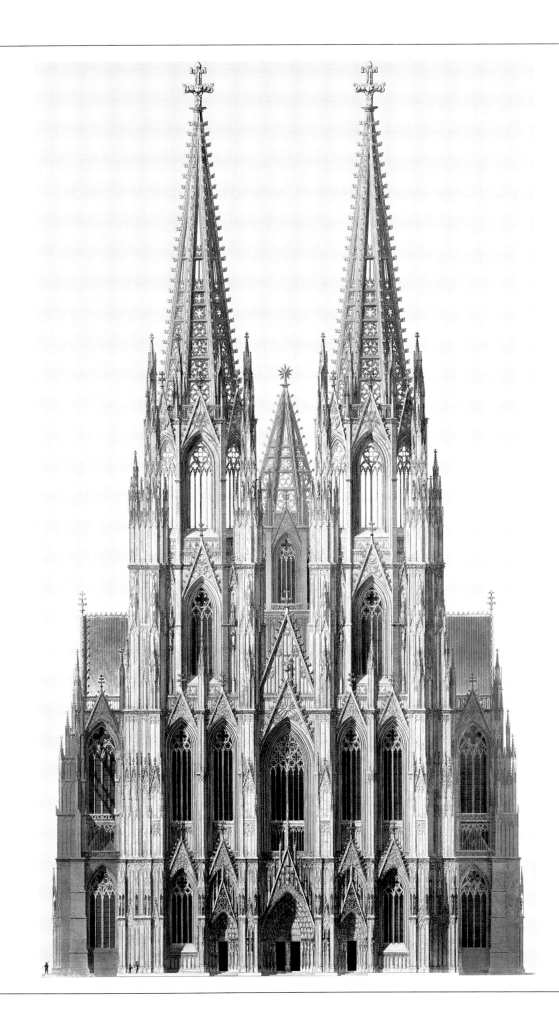

Arnold Wolff

The Cologne Cathedral

With Photos by Rainer Gaertner

Translated by Margret Maranuk-Rohmeder

VISTA POINT VERLAG

Front Cover: Cathedral of Cologne, West Façade
    Photo: Rainer Gaertner
Back Cover: Finial on the South Tower
    Photo: Rainer Gaertner
Front paper and end paper: The Medieval Façade Plan, c. 1300
    (Plan F), detail in a scale of 1:1
    Photo: Rainer Gaertner
Fronticepiece: 1 The West Façade of the Cathedral, Plate V from the
    engravings of the Cathedral by Sulpiz Boisserée, drawn in 1811 by
    M. H. Fuchs and in 1823 by Mauchert, engraved by Ernst Rauch, 1830
    Original: Verlag Kölner Dom
Page 1: Woodcut after a watercolor by Vincenz Statz
    »And finished it shall be!« (1861), from: *Deutsche Bauzeitung*, 1880

Deutsche Bibliothek Cataloguing-in-Publication Data

The Cologne cathedral / Arnold Wolff. With photos by Rainer
Gaertner. [Übers. ins Engl.: Margret Maranuk-Rohmeder]. –
Köln : Vista-Point-Verl., 1990
    Dt. Ausg. u.d.T.: Der gotische Dom in Köln
    ISBN 3-88973-105-8
NE: Wolff, Arnold [Mitverf.]; Gaertner, Rainer [Ill.]

© Vista Point Verlag, Cologne, 1990
All rights reserved
Photolithography: Industriedienst, Wiesbaden and Litho Köcher, Cologne
Typesetting and Printing: Rasch, Bramsche
Binding: Hunke & Schröder, Iserlohn
Printed in West Germany

ISBN 3-88973-105-8

Table of Contents

History and Description of the Cathedral of Cologne

2   South tower before 1842. Engraving by Wilhelm von Abbema, 1846, 79 × 63 cm/c. 31 × 24.5 in.

History and Description of the Cathedral of Cologne

Early Christian and Frankish Bishops in Cologne

The area over which the present Cathedral of Cologne rises constituted the northeast corner of the walled-in city in Roman times. In a normal house on a corner piece of property, 29 × 23.5 meters/95 × 77 feet, situated directly on the street along the wall, their eucharistic meeting room was located. Its well-preserved heating system could be found again while – doing archaeological excavations.

Following the Edict of Milan of 313 A. D., in which Emperor Constantine guaranteed religious freedom, this simple building was expanded to a church under the first bishop known by name, St. Maternus. To the east it was connected to an atrium, 80 meters/262 feet long, in front of which extended a house and a baptistry. The entire church complex was c. 130 meters/426 feet long.

Around 500 a small chapel was built in the middle of the atrium, in which two Franks of noble birth from the entourage of King Theudebert II, a woman and a boy, were buried around 550. The rich burial objects, discovered in 1959, are presently on exhibit in the Diözesan Museum.

Already a few years later, Bishop Carentinus (mentioned c. 565) expanded the church around the entire area of the atrium and extended it to a length of c. 85 meters/279 feet. To the west choir dating from the 4th century, which was dedicated to St. Peter and in which the horary prayer of the clergy decreed by Pope Gregory I (590–604) took place, the Choir of Mary in the east was added. According to the liturgical objects found there, it was mainly used for parish mass.

Shortly before 800 a further expansion added a new west coir with a ring-shaped atrium to it so that the ground plan became very similiar to the famous plan of the Cloister of St. Gallen.

3   Buildings of the Christian community at the end of the 4th century (suggestion for reconstruction): 1 pagan temple; 2 bishop's church; 3 atrium; 4 heatable building; 5 baptismal chapel

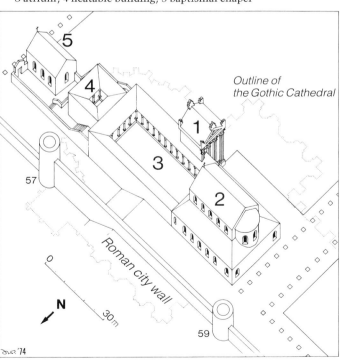

The Old Cathedral

Already at this time Archbishop Hildebold (c. 787–819) reigned, a friend and advisor of Charlemagne in all spiritual matters. The later oral history of Cologne made him responsible for having the Old Cathedral built. Nothing is recorded about the beginning of construction of this immense cathedral, already called the *mother and master of all churches in Germany* in the 13th century. Certain is merely that it was consecrated by Archbishop Willibert (870–889) on September 27, 870.

While in spite of intensive research, the shape and time of construction of earlier buildings still depend mainly on assumptions, there are not only a number of reports written about the Old Cathedral, but even a few pictures exist. The most important one is contained in the so-called *Hillinus Codex*, a valuable manuscript of the gospels, illuminated in Cologne by two monks from Reichenau around the year 1025. Above the scene showing the presentation of the manuscript to St. Peter, the patron of the Cathedral, a long

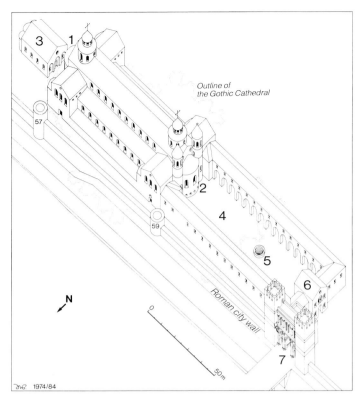

4　The Old Cathedral at the time of its consecration on September 27, 870. In the foreground is the Roman city wall of the 1st c. A.D. with the towers nos. 57 and 59 as well as the North Gate, situated along the *cardo maximus* (today the Hohe Strasse). 1 east choir; 2 west choir; 3 baptismal chapel; 4 west atrium; 5 fountain; 6 entrance gate; 7 Roman North Gate

5　The Old Cathedral. Suggestion for reconstruction for the ground plan toward the end of the 12th century: 1 Choir of St. Peter (west choir); 2 Choir of Mary (east choir); 3 nave, Altar of the Holy Cross; after 1164, Altar of the Three Magi; 4 west transept with apsidioles; 5 east transept with apsidioles; 6 inner side aisles, Carolingian; 7 outer side aisles, added under Archbishop Bruno (953–965); 8 west atrium, Carolingian; 9 Chapel of the Palatinate of Archbishop Heribert (999–1021); 10 east atrium of Archbishop Anno (1056–1075); 11 south entrance hall (known only from documents, no traces found). The Roman city wall of the 1st c. A.D. is marked with the letter T (T = tower), T 57, T 59, and the letter M (M = wall), M 58, markings introduced by Otto Doppelfeld.

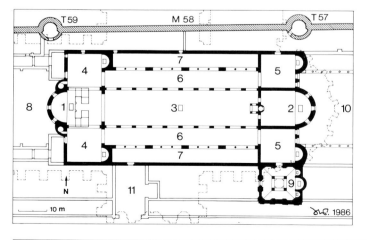

church building can be seen, which without doubt represents the Old Cathedral. This was impressively reinforced when the excavations under the Gothic Cathedral, begun in 1946, uncovered almost the entire foundation of the Old Cathedral.

The Old Cathedral acquired not only the entire length of its predecessor, c. 95 meters/311.5 feet, but also its basic shape. Here as there the Coir of St. Peter lay in the west and that of Mary in the east. In the central aisle was the nave, 12.4 meters/40.5 feet wide and four times as long; it was flanked by side aisles, half as wide as the nave. Transepts were located in the west as well as the east, which consisted of three bays, each the width of the nave. On their east sides were altogether four apsidioles. In the west there were two round bell towers situated in the corners between the apse and the transept walls. Towering over the roof of the nave were two large wooden crossing towers.

The choirs in the main apses were c. 2 meters/c. 6.5 feet higher than the floor in the nave. Under both were crypts. The west one, which is better known, was almost exactly like the crypt of Old St. Peter in Rome. In the west an atrium, 100 meters/328 feet long, was situated in front of it, which extended to the old Roman main street, today the Hohe Strasse. A deep well in its center can still be seen in the underground garage in front of the Cathedral.

Under the reign of Archbishop Bruno (953–965), the youngest brother of Emperor Otto the Great, the Cathedral experienced its first great alteration. He added a side aisle in both the north and the south, making the church five-aisled ever since, a mark of distinction which until then actually only befitted the churches of the Pope in Rome.

Soon thereafter Archbishop Gero (969–976) donated the *Gero Crucifix*, named after him, presently located in a Baroque altar frame dating from 1683 at the east end of the north side aisle. This Ottonian work of art is probably one of the oldest monumental sculptures of the Middle Ages still extant. During restoration in 1976 it was dendrochronologically determined that the oak from which the corpus is carved was no doubt felled during the lifetime of Archbishop Gero. Although this type of large-scale crucifix can already be found in Carolingian times, certain Byzantine characteristics are unmistakable in the Gero Crucifix. This is connected to the fact that Gero traveled to Constantinople in 971 to court Princess Theophanu for Otto II. As wife of Otto II, mother of Otto III, and regent of the empire, she became one of the most important women in the Middle Ages in Germany. The Gero Crucifix represents Christ as just deceased, thus capturing the moment of completed salvation. The corpus of Christ also loses none of its sovereign dignity in this realistic rendition of his horrible death on the cross. Thus, it is not surprising that this singular work of art found a wide, long-lasting following.

Gero was buried in the Cathedral in front of the crucifix which he had donated. Around 1265 his grave along with the tombstone was transferred to the Chapel of St. Stephen in the Gothic Cathedral. The tombstone was made of red sandstone with a tri-colored slab inlaid with white marble as well as red and green porphyry, materials obtained from wall panelings of Roman times.

Archbishop Heribert (999–1021), with whom the youthful Emperor Otto III was particularly closely associated, had the two-storied Chapel of the Palatinate built on the south end of the east transept. Its excavations can be seen in the courtyard of the cathedral workshop. The illumination in the Hillinus Codex shows the chapel rising like a tower on the right. Charlemagne's Palatinate Chapel in Aix-la-Chapelle served as a prototype, the ground plan of which, to be sure, was considerably simplified and reduced from eight to four supports.

Under Archbishop Anno (1056–1075) the Old Cathedral was connected by means of two high arcades with the collegiate church of St. Mary *ad gradus* (at the stairs) situated to the east. In 1981 one of the large red sandstone columns together with three bases was re-erected approximately on its original location.

In 1164 Archbishop Reinald von Dassel (1159–1167)

translated the mortal remains of the Three Magi from Milan to Cologne. They were placed in a wooden shrine composed of three regular shrines, two situated at the bottom and one on top. During the next six decades the shrine was covered by the best goldsmiths of the time with precious figures, jewels, and enamel plates. It is assumed that after c. 1181 Nikolaus of Verdun, the master of the Retable of Klosterneuburg, was in charge of the workshop. From this time originate the figures of the prophets on the lower long sides, which belong to the most remarkable accomplishments of sculpture at the end of the 12th century. After 1204 other masters finished the front with its figures chased from pure gold. The completion of the back with the Flagellation and Crucifixion of Christ took until c. 1225. Like a wonder this reliquiary shrine, the largest and most important of the Western World, survived the troublesome course of events, even though it had to suffer much demage and theft. Once the wooden core could no longer carry the incrustation, the goldsmiths Fritz Zehgruber and Peter Bolg restored the precious work between 1961 and 1973.

Immediately after the arrival of the relics of the Three Magi, Reinald von Dassel began to renovate the Old Cathedral. Through the addition of two towers in the east, the total number of towers was increased to six, all of which he had provided with domed roofs and golden orbs or crosses. Following the renovation out-

6 The Old Cathedral after modification by Archbishop Reinald von Dassel (1159–1167)

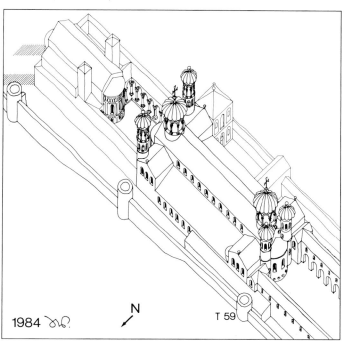

7 Construction site when the foundation stone was laid on August 15, 1248

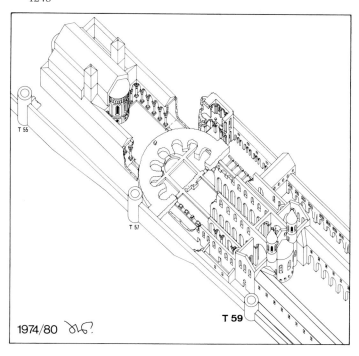

8   Vaulting of the chevet in Amiens (l.) and Cologne (r.). In Amiens the building elements coming from the vault crowd together on the narrow abacus of the capital. The purpose of the stocky columns (= old shafts), which encompass the core of the pillar, does not become apparent. In Cologne all members of the vault are given their logical support downward through the addition of more slender shafts (= new responds). The optically correct representation of the stream of thrust creates the impression of harmony and elegance.

side, the work inside was then completed by his successor, Philipp von Heinsberg (1167–1191). He had initially tried to hinder the citizens of Cologne from building a new wall, which they wanted in order to expand the area of the city from 100 to 400 hectare/247 to 988 acres. Following a bitter struggle and successful attempts at mediation through the emperor, he finally did approve construction of the wall. When Philipp's tomb was transferred from the Old Cathedral to the Chapel of St. Maternus in the Gothic Cathedral, c. 1300, it was given the shape of a city wall with towers and gates.

Pl 58

The Beginning of Construction of the Gothic Cathedral

Soon it became apparent that the Old Cathedral was no longer large enough to accomodate the throng of the ever-growing number of pilgrims, and also not the ambition of the archbishopric for it to be one of the most important in the empire. Archbishop Engelbert (1216–1225) urged the Chapter of the Cathedral to construct a new building and provided for considerable annual financial support. His murder on November 7, 1225, probably delayed the beginning of construction by years.

Toward the end of the year 1247, the Chapter of the Cathedral passed a formal resolution concerning the new building. Nevertheless, not until after the financing contract was passed on April 13, 1248, could work finally begin. Initially it was intended to demolish the east transept of the Old Cathedral so that the larger part could still be used as a bishop's church for many decades. However, uncautious demolition measures caused a fire on April 30, which burned down the entire Cathedral. Thereafter only the west half was provisionally restored and work was begun immediately on the foundation for the chapels of the chevet, eight to ten meters/26 to 33 feet deep. In a few months construction had proceeded far enough that Archbishop Konrad von Hochstaden (1238–1261)

7

could lay the foundation stone for the new Gothic building on August 15, 1248, the feast day of the Assumption of the Virgin.

While the masons' work now began on the seven chapels of the chevet, the foundation builders were already excavating the foundation holes for the south wall of the chevet and the east wall of the south transept. For the immense foundation walls, in addition to the debris from the Old Cathedral, columnar basalt blocks were used, which once paved the city streets in antique times and which in the course of thousands of years had shifted more to the disadvantage than to the benefit of traffic.

Master Gerhard

Such a construction site where over 100 people worked required cautious management. It was hard enough to solve the technical and organizational problems; it was even harder to answer the artistic questions. In the 19th century it was correctly assumed that the first master builder was a veritable genius. However, the medieval sources mention him merely as *Gerhard, the stonemason;* nevertheless, they accentuate his accomplishments. The Chapter of the Cathedral must have been very satisfied with his achievements, because in 1257 it signed over as an inheritable lease a piece of property, which was *wider and larger than usual* and upon which Gerhard had already built a stone house.

Without doubt, Gerhard had personally seen the great prototypes of the Cathedral in France, especially the Cathedral of Amiens. However, it is not likely that he had worked on them there, because otherwise he would have incorporated the technical innovations already customary there, and not, as comparative observations show, adhered to Romanesque building

9   Technical construction in the 13th century. On the left: upper side of a freestone from the buttressing of the chevet with traces of methods of production and transferral: 1 scratch line (axis of symmetry); 2 mark for the part of the building (square); 3 layer number (23); 4 hole for tongs, a similiar hole is also on the lower side; 5 hole for the lewis; 6 hole for the clamp with a slide-way for the cramp; 7 grooves for better adhesion of the mortar; 8 original outline of the freestone. – Center: large stone tongs. – On the right: spreading lewis, below in the same scale as the tongs; above is a sectional drawing with the hole for the lewis.

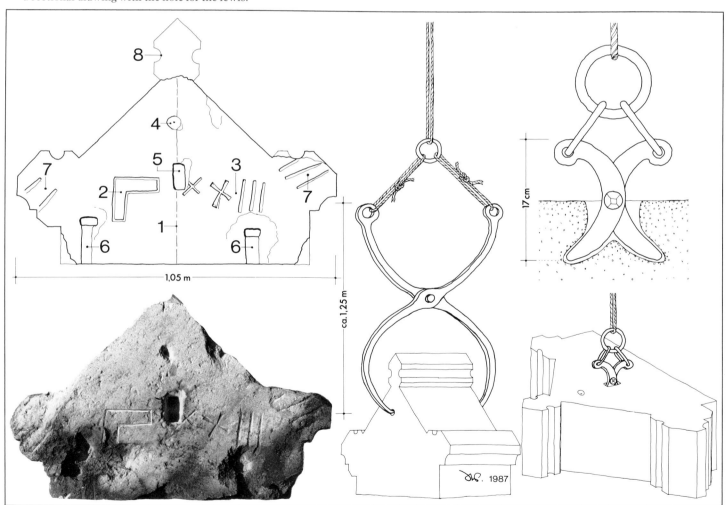

practices. Yet Gerhard was less interested in technical construction and much more interested in art. He grasped the highly developed design of the Cathedral of Amiens, discovered the last aesthetic insufficiencies still inherent in it, and successfully avoided them in Cologne. He refined the articulation of the interior 8 with its vault ribs and pillar responds to its highest perfection, thus completing the Cathedral as a type of building. Further enhancement was not possible and was also not attempted again.

Even if the Cologne stonemasons did not achieve the technical niveau of their French colleagues, nonetheless, their ability as craftsmen surpassed that of the local level. In the Romanesque churches only the piers, arches, and cornices were assembled out of carved workpieces, everything else was constructed of soft tuff; thereafter all surfaces were covered with a thin layer of mortar. In contrast, on the Cathedral all visible parts are constructed of large hewn freestones cut from the stone, so-called *trachyte,* from the Drachenfels located 40 kilometers upstream. With the help of lists, the freestones were roughly hewn, dragged down a sloping plain to the nearby bank of the Rhine River, and brought via ships to Cologne.

Probably about 25 stonemasons worked in the workshop. Since a certain amount of time elapsed between quarrying and setting the stones in place, the finished workpieces had to be stored, which in turn 9 made exact marking necessary. In Cologne each part of the building was given its own mark, i. e., a half-moon, a linden leaf, or a square. In addition, the number of the stone layer was struck in it in Roman numerals. All the markings were carved on inside surfaces so that they later disappeared in the wall and were no longer visible. Only much later were the small marks of stonemasons added, which can often be seen carved in the visible surfaces and which only reveal something about the craftsmen who did the work, but which have nothing to do with the location markings described here.

To transport the stones huge iron tongs were used, which grasped the stones from two sides so that they could be transferred. To prevent the stones from slipping out during transport, small holes were struck into the sides, into which the pointed arms of the tongs could grip. Such holes can still be seen today on many old buildings. In Cologne it was soon regretted that the beautiful, carefully faced stones carved with such great effort were ruined by such ugly holes, only in use for a few minutes. From the second stage of building on, they were only struck into the inside surfaces. This then had the disadvantage that the stones could no longer simply be lowered onto the layer below. Therefore, the tongs were now only used for heavy

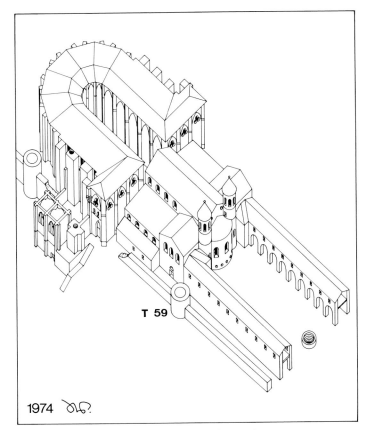

10   Stage of construction of the Cathedral around 1265

lifting. To actually put the stones in place, a second lifting device was used, the so-called lewis, which grasped into the stones from above. Already in general use in antiquity, such instruments existed in several variations. In Cologne it looked like inverted tongs, the arms of which didn't close when you drew on the handles, but rather spread open. With a few carefully aimed blows, the stonemasons struck a hole into the 9 center of gravity of the stone from above as exactly as possible, into which the spreading lewis, specially blacksmithed for this purpose, fit exactly. This made it possible to raise and lower a stone any number of times without difficulty.

This was also necessary since the heavy parts, often weighing over 400 kilograms/880 pounds, could not be layered in a prepared bed of mortar and be hammered until they fit in place like the small stones in Romanesque churches. Instead, the freestones were lowered onto thin wedges of wood having the exact thickness of the subsequent mortar joints, mostly four to six millimeters. Then it was checked whether the stone fit correctly, which was naturally most often not the case. If not, it had to be lifted again and the small pieces of wood had to be carved thinner or be underlaid thicker. When the piece fit exactly enough, then the joints were closed off with clay and liquid mortar was poured in. For the tracery in the windows and free-standing pinnacles, heated lead was used, which also covered the wrought-iron dowels interconnecting the stones.

With all respect to the manual abilities of the stonemasons, nevertheless, the greatest admiration should be extended to the accomplishments of the master builders, because they united all these activities, guiding and managing. From the design until completion, they always had to keep the final aim in mind, the perfect cathedral. They had to carry the responsibility for a highly costly building operation, which might appear simple to us today, but which in the Middle Ages, when all this was being tried out for the first time, must have been shockingly different and, therefore, required a master who was far ahead of his times. He constantly had to make new discoveries, develop new forms of organization, and track down new possibilities of economizing and of making artistric innovations. Therefore, it is not surprising that legends were spun around these heroic figures, of which Gerhard was certainly the most outstanding, connecting them with using devilish tricks, since for simple people that which was accomplished on such a cathedral building could have only have been possible if the devil had been involved.

12 Dormition of the Virgin. A wall painting in the Chapel of Our Lady, c. 1265 (not visible to the public).

11 A grisaille window from a chapel in the chevet. Following a tracing of the original by architect Wilhelm Hoffmann (1845), the panel was reconstructed in 1984 and installed in the Chapel of St. Stephen.

Construction of the Chevet

Master Gerhard probably died around 1260. By this time the axial chapel and the adjacent Chapel of St. John were probably already finished and the rest of the chapels of the chevet were under construction. Management of construction was then assigned to the second master, whose name comes down to us as Arnold. Although he is first mentioned in documents in 1271, it is hardly likely that another master existed about whom nothing is known.   Pl 6, 11

Excluding the transept façades Arnold, whose period in office lasted until at least 1299, finished within a few years the ground floor of the chevet, which could already be used between 1265 and 1270.   10 Via a high staircase he joined the inner side aisles of the Old Cathedral with those of the Gothic chevet so that processions became possible through both parts of the church. He had the open ends of the transepts and arcades toward the inner choir closed off by walls.

From the earliest decoration with wall paintings, a fragment of the Dormition of the Virgin is extant,   12 which, however, is not visible to the public. The chapel windows in the chevet were glazed with fanciful designs of leaf tendrils done in grisaille (untinted glass), particularly well known from the churches of the Cistercians, i.e., in Altenberg near Cologne.

11 Unfortunately, all the original grisailles of the Cathedral were lost. In recent years some have been reconstructed based on tracings and existing fragments. They are installed in the Chapel of St. John and the Chapel of St. Stephen.

The only stained-glass window still extant from the earliest decoration is the central window in the axial chapel, the so-called »Elder Biblical Window« dating from around 1260, the style of which can still be designated as Late Romanesque. In the right light it shows scenes from the life of Christ and in the left light the corresponding Old Testament prefigurations are placed next to them.

Pl 49–52

13, 14 In 1277 the square hall of the sacristy was consecrated, a particularly elegant architectural entity, the

14 Chapel of the Holy Sacrament, formerly the chapter hall or sacristy

13 Sectional drawing of the Chapel of the Holy Sacrament and the north section of the chevet in its condition before 1868: 1 moat of the Roman city wall; 2 Roman city wall, 1st c. A.D.; 3 upward sloping area to the south; 4 north outer wall of the Old Cathedral, 9th c.; 5 Gothic foundation of a pier, 13th c., dotted because it lies behind the area of the cutaway; 6 foundation of the wall on the north side of the chevet of the Gothic Cathedral; 7 basement under the Chapel of the Holy Sacrament before installation of the intermediate brick vault; 8 former sacristy north building (archive and treasury), razed 1868; 9 Chapel of the Holy Sacrament, originally the chapter hall, since 1580 the sacristy, consecrated in 1277; 10 atrium between the Cathedral and the Chapel of the Holy Sacrament; 11 cell, probably a guard room, above the atrium; a ground level in Roman times; b floor level of the Old Cathedral; c ground level outside in Gothic times; d present ground level outside

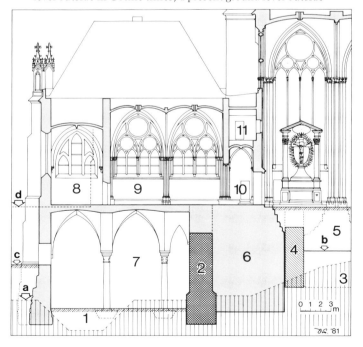

construction of which must have caused considerable technical difficulties. On the other side of the Roman wall located approximately where the north wall of the side aisle of the chevet would be, the ground sloped steeply downward. In order to reach the floor level of the Cathedral, it was first necessary to build a basement, 10.5 meters/34.5 feet high. Today used as a sacristy (the Chapel of the Holy Sacrament), its four vaults rest upon a slender monolithic pillar. It appears that it was originally the chapter hall, in which the collegiate clergymen congregated to make important decisions, i.e., to elect a new archbishop.

15 At about the same time, the upper choir with its fifteen enormous clerestory windows and its famous buttressing was completed. The vaulting was closed off at a height of 43.35 meters/142 feet. Over it rises the steep roof, the roof ridge of which is crowned by open tracery cresting with guilded lilies, terminating 61.1 meters/200 feet above the floor. Toward the west the chevet was closed off in its full height by a provisional separating wall, which was finished at the latest by 1304 and which remained standing until 1863.

Pl 5, 6
Pl 9
Pl 17, 18
Pl 61

Decoration of the Chevet

Pl 10

Pl 17

Pl 47

Now it was time to finish the decoration of the chevet. By around 1310 the *glass-paintings* in the windows in the upper choir, 17.15 meters/56 feet high, were probably finished. In the lower third a total of 48 kings stand on consoles with the coats of arms of their donors from the nobility of the Rhineland and the eminent families of Cologne patricians. It is assumed that the kings, portrayed alternately with and without beards, represent the kings of Judea, the Old Testament ancestors of Christ, and the 24 elders of the Apocalypse according to St. John. In the central window the Adoration of the Three Magi can be recognized. Above this scene kings and prophets appear alternately upward into the zone of tracery. Nonetheless, only in this central window are there stained-glass figures; all of the other windows have richly composed panels of carpet designs in muted, constantly changing tones. With 850 square meters/1016.5 square yards of surface, this cycle of glass-painting is the largest one still extant from the first half of the 14th century. More than 95 percent of the glass still belongs to the time of construction. Unfortunately, many pieces are severely damaged by weath-

1974

15 Stage of construction of the Cathedral when the chevet was consecrated on September 27, 1322

16 »Madonna of Milan« in the Chapel of Our Lady, end of the 13th c.

17   A leaf-mask, a miseracord on the choir stalls

18   Lovers, a miseracord on the choir stalls

of Christ are represented, just as scenes from antique sagas and popular belief. The Chapter of the Cathedral sat here while fulfilling its most noble task, i. e., singing psalms to honor God.

Behind the choir stalls rise the choir screens, which are decorated on the inside with *cycles of pictures.* On the north side they show stories of St. Peter, Pope Sylvester, and Emperor Constantine; in the south appear the Life of the Virgin, the story of the Three Magi up to the arrival of their remains in Cologne, and the legends of Sts. Felix and Nabor, the relics of whom are also preserved in the Shrine of the Three Magi. Under the 42 large pictures on the north side is a complete row of archbishops from Cologne, while on the south side the emperors of the Roman and German empires are painted, an allusion to the dual function of the Archbishop of Cologne, who combined the religious position of being the head shepherd with the worldly job of being an Electoral Prince. Paul Clemen called these paintings, done between 1332 and 1340, *the most important work for the art to come and the best in quality within German monumental painting of the 14th century.* Pl 8, 15 Pl 33 Pl 38–43

Statues of *Christ and Virgin Mary* as well as the *twelve apostles* stand on foliated consoles against the pillars in the choir. Over them rise high canopies, crowned by angels with musical instruments. Only over Christ and the Virgin rise purely architectonic elements. The statues, carved 1280–1290, show the sculptural art of the Cologne cathedral workshop at its best at the time of Master Builder Arnold. The material is fine tuff with a rich polychromy, renewed in 1840, which deserves special attention in particular due to its 39 different patterns of fabric. A related work in wood carved at about the same time is the »Madonna of Milan« in the Chapel of Our Lady, much endeared to the citizens of Cologne. Pl 45, 46, 6 16

On September 27, 1322, the Chapter of the Cathedral finally moved into the new chevet after 74 years of construction. The Shrine of the Three Magi was also transferred and found its place in the axial chapel, from which the tomb of Archbishop Konrad dating from 1261 had to be relocated to the Chapel of St. John. All of the windows in the ambulatory, which until then had grisaille glass with the exception of the Biblical Window in the axial chapel, were glazed with stained-glass paintings in the lower third based on the model of the clerestory windows in the upper choir, from which the *Window of the Three Magi,* among others, is still extant. Pl 28 25 Pl 53, 54

On the same day the *high altar* was consecrated, one of the largest in all of Christianity. The altar slab consists of a monolithic, pitch-black marble block, measuring 4.52 × 2.12 meters/15 × 7 feet. Weighing Pl 44

ering, broken, or dirty so that the windows had to be restored with great diligence. Until the 18th century the same design was in the window in the triforium as in the corresponding window above it. In time this state will be restored, as it already is in the first windows in the north side of the choir.

Around 1311 the *choir stalls,* already begun around 1308, were installed. Consisting of 104 seats they are the largest in Germany. The ends and the aisles to the upper rows of seats are decorated with richly carved bench ends. Between the individual seats are expressively carved grotesques with foliage-work, animals, and people. However, the misericords, which cannot be seen until the seats are clapped up, are the main decoration. Here people, animals, and fable creatures can be seen, not only dancing, fighting, and singing, but also begging, scoffing, and showing affection. Scenes from the Old Testament and from the parables Pl 8 Pl 33–37 Pl 61 17, 18

about 6.7 tons it is the largest stone in the Cathedral. In the white marble arcading on the walls, the apostles stand, flanking the central scene of Christ Crowning the Virgin on the front.

Construction of the Western Parts

It appears that the construction of the south tower had already begun before the chevet was consecrated. For it the parchment plan, measuring 4.05 × 1.7 meters/ 13 × 5.5 feet, was probably drawn around 1300, which presently hangs in the Chapel of St. John. The master builder at this time was John, the son of Arnold, whose activity can be traced after 1296 and who was followed by Rutger from 1331 to 1333.

A report about the demolition of an entrance hall of the Old Cathedral in use until then leads to the conclusion that the foundations for the south side aisles were laid in 1325. The piers and walls were built up over the height of the capitals (c. 13.5 meters/44 feet), 19 the entire section of the building including the south transept was roofed over by three parallel saddle roofs, and the openings toward the nave were walled up. Thus, mass could be performed in the entire south

19 Stage of construction of the Cathedral when the university was founded on January 7, 1389

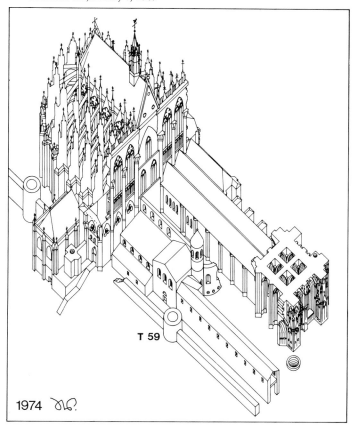

T 59

1974

20 Portal of St. Peter, the head of St. Peter, c. 1375

area at the latest for the celebration of the founding of the University of Cologne on January 7, 1389.

The master builder at this time was Michael (1353–c. 1395). His daughter married Heinrich von Gmünd, a close relative of Peter Parler, who was called from Cologne to Prague as master builder in 1353. The close relations to Bohemia are also expressed in the art works of this epoch, especially on the Portal of St. 20 Peter (c. 1370–1380), the only one of the nine portals to Pl 21, 22 be completed in the Middle Ages. The five large jamb statues of the apostles Peter, Andrew, and James (on the left) as well as Paul and John (on the right), just as the 34 seated statues of the angels, prophets, and saints in the archivolts, have been replaced by cast stone copies. The originals are located in the Diözesan Museum. Only the tympanum relief over the door with the condemnation and the martyrdom of Sts. Peter and Paul remained in place.

Begun around the same time, the second floor of the powerful south tower already shows considerable 2 deviation from the large façade plan. It was probably completed under the direction of Master Builder

Pl 12, 13 Andreas von Everdingen (c. 1395–1411). The inside, extremely carefully furnished architectonically, was filled with an immense belfry until 1876, in which the two large bells, Pretiosa and Speciosa were hung in 1448 and 1449. Together with the Bell of the Three Magi, already cast in 1414, they create a unique peal with the striking tones G-A-B, famous far and wide, which can still be heard on certain days. Since 1923 the peal has been supplemented lower on the scale by

Pl 94 the immense bell of St. Peter, while the bells of the 19th and 20th centuries have complemented it higher on the scale.

Pl 20, 83 The third floor was built up to above the window ledges before building operations ceased. The building crane protruding from the provisional roof was left standing. It became a landmark of Cologne and proof that construction on the Cathedral had not stopped altogether, but was merely interrupted.

In the 15th century construction was directed by Master Nikolaus von Büren (1425–1445), his son-in-law Konrad Kuene (1445–1469), and Johannes von 22, 23 Frankenberg (until 1491). At this time construction

continued on the north side, where the east wall of the Pl 16, 20, 68 tower was built up to a height of 28 meters/92 feet, and 23 the six west side aisle bays including the vault were completed. However, the six bays in the east just as the ones on the south side were built up only 13.5 meters/44 feet high. Also these parts of the building were covered over along with the crossing and the transept by low roofs. When building operations permanently shut down, 90 percent of the planned ground area of the Cathedral was roofed over, but only the chevet had reached its full height.

Works of Art of the Late Gothic Period

In the years 1508/09 a cycle of magnificent Renaissance *stained-glass paintings* were installed in the five windows in the north side aisle. The donors were the archbishops Hermann IV von Hessen (1480–1508), his successor Philipp II von Daun (1508–1515) with Pl 56 his relatives, and the city of Cologne, represented by four knights as saints below the scene of the Nativity.

21 Cathedral and cathedral square (today Roncalliplatz) in 1798, drawn by L. Janscha, engraved by F. Ziegler, water-colored engraving, 28.9 × 43.8 cm/c. 11 × 17 in.; from *50 malerische Ansichten des Rheinstromes von Speyer bis Düsseldorf*, Vienna, 1798

In the lowest row appear Marcus Vipsanius Agrippa
Pl 55   (62–12 B. C.), the founder of the city, and Marsilius, a
hero from a saga from earlier times, each with a banner
on which the golden crowns of the Three Magi radiate
against the red background. The fame of these five
windows rests not only on the high-quality artistic
designs, made by the best artists of the Cologne School
of Painting, but also on the extremely masterly execution of the stained-glass in the workshop of Hermann
Pentelynck.

Pl 57   Among the *grave monuments* the one of Count
Gottfried von Arnsberg († 1372) deserves special attention. He was buried in the Cathedral because he
bequeathed his county to the Archbishopric of Cologne. Prior to this he had donated rich gifts to the
community of Neheim, the citizens of which even
today annually bring a wreath to his grave. The recum-
bent effigy of hard syenite portrays the count in a suit
of armor, full of detail and with the realistic features of
the deceased. Traces of the former life-like polychromy can still be detected. The grating supposedly
was mounted to protect the effigy from enraged
relatives, who felt themselves passed over by the in-
heritance.

Against the pillar rising up behind the tomb stands a
Pl 59   mighty *Statue of St. Christopher*, 3.73 meters/12 feet
high, carrying Infant Jesus through an agitated body of
water. The sculpture carved of tuff, the polychromy of
which was renewed following old traces, is attributed
to the sculptor Tilman von der Burch.

On the opposite pillar a particularly lovely small
Pl 60   statue of the *Virgin with Child* can be seen. It belongs
to the so-called »Beautiful Madonnas« of the »Soft
Style«, which were very popular from 1380 to 1420.

Among the numerous works of art of this epoch
which were not produced for the Cathedral, but which
later found their home here, there are four large altar-
Pl 62, 63   pieces. The oldest of them is the *Altarpiece of St.
Clare*, the largest and artistically most important
altarpiece of Cologne in the 14th century and the oldest altogether with an eucharistic tabernacle incorporated in it. It was commissioned in 1350 for the
Church of the Poor Clares, which was razed in 1804.
Completely opened it shows superb statues of Christ
and the twelve apostles above reliquiary busts of the
virgins of St. Ursula. Upon the first closing, there are
24 paintings with scenes from the Youth (below) and
the Passion (above) of Christ. These pictures were
painted over around 1400; however, the ones on the
outer wings were laid free around 1900 so that today
both epochs of style can be seen next to one another.

Pl 64, 65   World famous is the *Altarpiece of the City Patrons*,
also called the *Cathedral Altarpiece*, which Stephan
Lochner painted c. 1445, commissioned by the City of

22   Crown of an arch on the Late Gothic arcade in the north side aisle
of the nave with crossing moldings, c. 1510–1560

23   Stage of construction of the Cathedral when building operations
ceased in 1560

Cologne for the Council Chapel. It was not only the spiritual center of Cologne as a political entity, which practically represented a republic directly connected to the Empire, but also the main work of the Cologne School of Painting. Just as in the »Maesta« paintings in the town halls of the rich northern Italian cities, the citizens here honor their Lord by allowing themselves to be represented by the patron saints of the city at the heavenly court. On the wings approach the age-old patrons, crowds of martyrs associated with Sts. Ursula and Gereon. The central panel, dominated by the Virgin Enthroned, shows the Adoration of the Three Magi, the relicts of whom have rested in the Cathedral since 1164. In contrast to the colorful inside, 5.22 meters/17 feet wide, the gilding of which is even more enhanced by the sculptural band of tracery arcades representing heaven, the Annunciation is painted in muted tones on the outside and is set in a vertical black frame. After the Council Chapel was closed during the French occupation (1794–1815) and the altarpiece was hidden in a cellar, it was brought into the Cathedral in 1809, where it soon elicited the admiration of art connoisseurs. However, not until it was mounted behind the altar in the Chapel of Our Lady did it regain its original function as a devotional image in 1950.

Pl 67   The *Altarpiece of Agilolphus* also entered the Cathedral in the early 19th century. Originally it was located to the east of the Cathedral in the Church of St. Mary *ad gradus* (at the stairs), which was razed in 1817. This altarpiece, remarkable for its size (6.8 meters/22 feet wide and 5.5 meters/18 feet high), was produced in a workshop in Antwerp in 1521. In the carved central shrine, the Deposition and Lamentation are surrounded by other scenes from the Passion. On the precious painted wings, the lives of the canonized Cologne bishops Agilolphus (c. 748) and Anno II (1056–1075) are shown, statues of whom crown the work flanking the central Madonna.

Pl 66   Not until 1960 did an *Altarpiece of the Three Magi* enter the Cathedral, which was painted in Antwerp in 1520 for the Cloister of Bethlehem near Charleville (Belgium) and which is presently hanging in the Chapel of St. Maternus. It is a type of triptych, but all three parts are painted on a single panel, 2.25 meters/ c.7.5 feet wide. In spite of the abundance of objects spread out among the figures, the painting radiates an elevated solemnity.

A Long Pause

It seems that the Chapter of the Cathedral resigned itself to the fact that the Cathedral would remain unfinished. The use of the altar by several vicars of the Cathedral was justified by the reference to the upcoming completion, but no activities have been recorded. It was the travelers, the historians, and the theologians, who, on the one hand, praised the unheard-of artistic quality of the Cathedral, and, on the other hand, regretted the incomplete state, calling for resumption of work. In contrast, the Chapter of the Cathedral was content if it could raise the money for the current maintenance of the many roofs and eaves troughs. Larger projects, like the renewel of the ridge turret in Baroque forms in 1744, depended on subsidies granted by the archbishop, who also financed the greatest part of the costs for lining the open framework in the nave and transept with a wooden vault and for whitewashing the entire interior including many wall paintings, which was carried out by Italian specialists.   21

Nevertheless, even during these times a few furnishings of high quality entered the Cathedral. Around 1688 Cardinal Wilhelm Egon von Fürstenberg, a candidate for the throne of the archbishop (which he nonetheless did not attain), donated to the Cathedral eight valuable *gobelins* made according to   Pl 72 cartoons by Peter Paul Rubens. They were supposed to cover up the choir screens, the medieval paintings on which had become homely to look at, and represented the Triumph of the Holy Eucharist over the Old Testament, heresy, disbelief, and wordly science. In time they faded considerably, were taken down and poorly stored so that they had to be restored from 1975 to 1984. Every year around Pentecost they are hung up along the arcades in the nave for about six weeks.

Upon the initiative and probably also at the expense of the Canon Heinrich Mering (1620–1700), the Gero   Pl 26 Crucifix was framed by a marble altar screen in 1683. In addition, the grating covering the Shrine of the   Pl 28 Three Magi had to yield to a marble mausoleum, the façade of which is presently erected as an altar in the north transept. From 1769 on the medieval furnishings of the chevet were demolished and replaced by new altars and gratings in Early Classicist style.

In 1794 the French seized Cologne. The archbishop and the Chapter of the Cathedral fled; the Cathedral was closed and used for profane purposes for many years. In 1801 it was re-opened for church services as a parish church; nevertheless, the seat of the bishopric had been moved to Aix-la-Chapelle.

In these times of deepest degradation, enthusiasm for this singular building began to rekindle. Georg Forster (1790) and Friedrich von Schlegel (1804) praised it as a singular work of art, Joseph Görres as a   Pl 77 national shrine (1814). Practical work, however, was only carried out by Sulpiz Boisserée (1783–1856), who

24 Sectional drawing of the chevet of the Cathedral. Plate VI from the engravings of the Cathedral by Sulpiz Boisserée; drawn by Maximilian Fuchs, 1809; engraved by Christian Duttenhofer, 1811–1814, size of the pl, 79.5 × 53 cm/c. 31 × 20.5 in.

25 Epitaph of Archbishop Konrad von Hochstaden (1238–1261) in the Chapel of St. John; after an engraving by J. Hoffmann and C. Moisy (1811–1823) from the engravings of the Cathedral by Boisserée

began from 1808 on to record the Cathedral in drawings and never grew tired of promoting its completion. In his monumental series of engravings, »Views, Plans and Individual Parts of the Cathedral of Cologne...«, published between 1821 and 1832, he familiarized the public with his solicitations. He managed to interest Goethe, King Ludwig I of Bavaria, and finally also the young Crown Prince of Prussia in the Cathedral, before he could yet imagine what a decisive role the latter in particular would play in future developments. 1, 24, 25

Through the resolution passed by the Vienese Congress, the Rhineland and with it also Cologne, was incorporated by the Kingdom of Prussia after the defeat of Napoleon in 1815. It immediately began negotiations with the Pope aimed at reinstating Cologne as an archbishopric. Thereby, the Prussian government assumed the financial obligation for the maintenance of the bishop's church. After Karl Friedrich Schinkel as chief architect of Prussia visited the Cathedral already in 1816 and demanded urgent repairs, practical work finally began in 1823 by establishing a new cathedral workshop, which immediately undertook repairing the roofs, but then soon began tally and stonemasons' work. Pl 18

In 1833 Schinkel sent the most talented Silesian architect, Ernst Friedrich Zwirner (1802–1861), as cathedral architect to Cologne. He immediately began to draw up plans for finishing the Cathedral and to determine costs. At the same time he had the buttressing on the chevet restored. The original struts, which were extremely finely proportioned, were renewed in clearly stronger yet clumsier forms. Pl 6

Further Construction Following the Original Plan

Under the frugal King Friedrich Wilhelm III, who reigned from 1797 on, continuation of construction financed by the government was not feasible. Not until Friedrich Wilhelm IV, the *romantic on the throne*, came to power in November, 1840, did new hopes begin to germinate. The citizens of Cologne founded the Friends of the Cathedral Society *(Zentral-Dombau-Verein)*, which the King approved under the condition that it match funds with the allotment of the government for the Cathedral. A sum of 50,000 taler annually was agreed upon. Pl 82

On September 4, 1842, the moment was ripe. During the first of many festivals for the construction of the Cathedral in the 19th century, the King personally came to Cologne and together with Archbishop Johannes von Geissel (1841–1864) laid the foundation stone to recommence construction on the west pier of the south transept façade.

The plans as approved by the King intended to erect the nave and transept without the expensive buttressing. However, the Friends of the Cathedral Society didn't want to accept this. It pointed out that the King by approving the statute which explicitly emphasized construction *following the original plan* had also committed himself to the buttressing. The King finally gave in, which was not difficult for him personally, and Zwirner could expand his plans for the construction of the buttressing.

Pl 19

However, the first task was to build the transept Pl 80, 82 façades, for which no medieval plans existed. Zwirner drew them up completely new based on elements of the large façade plan and the finished parts of the south tower, constantly collaborating with Schinkel, Boisserée, and the King. When on the north side a fragment Pl 81 of a façade came to light from under the rubble and ruins, which deviated considerably from the project already under construction by Zwirner on the south side, the Friends of the Cathedral Society demanded that these parts be razed and a new façade be produced based on the uncovered fragment. Zwirner immediately drew such a plan, but the King curtailed the bitterly raging fight by wisely deciding that both designs

26 In the style of a medieval master builder, Richard Voigtel (cathedral architect, 1861–1902) had himself portrayed as a console figure in the first gallery on the north tower in 1870.

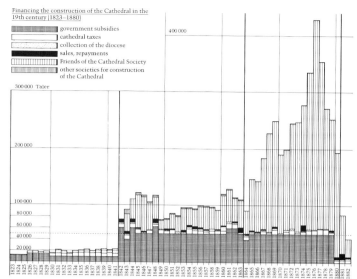

Financing the construction of the Cathedral in the 19th century (1823–1880)

- government subsidies
- cathedral taxes
- collection of the diocese
- sales, repayments
- Friends of the Cathedral Society
- other societies for construction of the Cathedral

The chart visualizes how variegated the financing of the construction of the Cathedral was in the 19th century. In spite of practically non-fluctuating government subsidies, the share of which to be sure decreased in proportion to the whole in the third stage of construction, the planning authorities constantly had to anticipate unexpected collapses. Every political and economic crisis left its mark overly clearly on the income of the Society. The following table shows how differently the main financial supporters were involved in the three stages of construction (all money is converted to taler)

	1823–1841	1842–1863	1864–1880	1823–1880
total expenditures	357272	2215824	4054939	6628035
government subsidies	60,4 %	51,5 %	19,5 %	32,4 %
cathedral taxes and collections	38,7 %	8,0 %	3,3 %	6,8 %
societies	–,–	37,9 %	76,5 %	59,4 %
other	0,9 %	2,6 %	0,7 %	1,4 %

27 Statistics for financing the construction of the Cathedral

should be carried out. This is how the Cathedral came to benefit from two different transept façades: one on the north side corresponding to the medieval plan and one on the south side following the purely Neo-Gothic Pl 4 design of Zwirner.

For the Festival for the Construction of the Cathedral in 1848, which in spite of political chaos and great financial distress was celebrated at considerable expense, all the side aisles and the nave were built up to just above the triforium. The height of the interior, 27 meters/88.5 feet, was now twice as high as before 1842. Then the transept façades shot upwards, 70 meters/c. 230 feet high. The King saw the Cathedral for the last time when he attended the ceremonious mounting of the cruciform foliated finial on the south Pl 82, 83 gable on October 3, 1855. In 1861 the roof with its crossing tower, 109 meters/357.5 feet high, was finished and two years later the entire interior was opened for church services. Finally, the large separating wall, which closed off the chevet toward the west Pl 8, 9, 14, 68 for 560 years, could be taken down. However, the three people who had most eagerly yearned for this day did not experience it: Boisserée had already died in 1854; Zwirner and the King followed him in 1861.

26 Richard Voigtel from Magdeburg, who had been actively involved in building the Cathedral since 1855, became the new cathedral architect. In order to counter ever-increasing worries about adequate funding, the Friends of the Cathedral Society sponsored an

27 annual lottery for the construction of the Cathedral after 1864, sanctioned by the government, which soon brought in considerable income. The powerful towers, 157 meters/515 feet high, could thus be completed in

Pl 84, 85 merely 17 years. In 1868 the north tower had reached the height of the south tower and the old crane, a landmark of the city of Cologne, had to yield to the progress of the building, which was regretted by many. When on October 15, 1880, the last stone was placed

28, 29 on the cruciform foliated finial on the south tower, the citizens of Cologne could after 632 years celebrate completion of their Cathedral in the presence of

Pl 1, 2 Emperor Wilhelm I.

19th-Century Works of Art

Although the government only provided for the sheer costs of construction, the number of works of art could also be increased in the 19th century by many new

28 View into the openwork tracery spire of the northwest tower, built 1877–1880

29 The document for the completion of the Cathedral is placed in the cruciform foliated finial. Woodcut from the *Allgemeine Illustrirte Zeitung*

additions exclusively financed by private donations. Schinkel already collected money at the court in Berlin for the *twelve angels* in the open pinnacles on the Pl 88 exterior of the chevet. They were carved following his designs by the Cologne sculptor W. J. Imhoff between 1834 and 1841 and are among the best Classicist sculptures in Germany.

From 1843 to 1845 the Nazarene Edward von Steinle painted magnificent *figures of angels* in the spandrels Pl 15, 17 of the arcade in the choir using the technique of fresco in order to replace the medieval originals, which were severely damaged and which were beginning to show through the Baroque withewash. Soon thereafter Friedrich Overbeck began in Rome to work on a large painting of the *Assumption of the Virgin*, mounted in Pl 73 the Cathedral in 1854 and presently hanging on the south wall in the transept.

Already in 1842 King Ludwig I of Bavaria donated the five *windows* in the south side aisle, which were Pl 76 manufactured in the Royal Factory for Stained Glass in Munich and installed in 1848. They encompass a concise history of salvation from the Baptism of John via the three great godly events, the Nativity, the Passion, the Descent of the Holy Ghost, to the Martyrdom of St. Stephen. The best and most famous masters of the Munich School collaborated on this unique cycle, artistically indeed the most important work of its kind in the 19th century. The overall concept of content and formal composition must have been based almost exclusively on ideas of Sulpiz Boisserée.

Pl 77   In 1854 the same workshop also manufactured the Görres' window to honor the great publicist and teacher Joseph Görres, which following severe damage by war was restored and re-installed in the south transept in 1980. Next to it the window with the representation of the Council of the Apostles in Jerusalem can be seen. Unfortunately, most of the stained-glass paintings manufactured in the 19th century were destroyed by war. The large west window by Julius Milde fortunately remained intact and is awaiting reinstallment in its original location.

Pl 4, 86   To obtain designs for the sculptural decoration of the nine large portals, the Munich sculptor Ludwig Schwanthaler was commissioned to prepare sketches. After his death in 1847, the execution was entrusted to Christian Mohr, who created all the *sculptures on the south portals.* He retained the overall composition of Schwanthaler, but changed his Classicist contour of line to that of Nazarene/Neo-Gothic style. The gentle sadness, particularly characteristic of the large statues, reminds us of the art of Friedrich Overbeck.

Pl 1, 89   The two other *portal façades* were decorated from c. 1868 to 1882 almost entirely with sculptures by Peter Fuchs, whose late style appealed to the realistic taste for art in the time after the Empire was founded. He was less sensitive than Mohr, but much more willing to follow the wishes of his patrons. The language of his Pl 92, 93 forms, which was full of variation in the beginning, gradually became duller and more formalistic, which is hardly surprising considering the almost series-like production of about 700 statues.

Thus, it was only consequent that Fuchs was passed over for the design of the *bronze portals* and that younger artists were engaged. From 1883 to 1890 Hugo Schneider created the leaves of the doors on the south side, which were unfortunately destroyed in the war, as well as those on the west side. Their fanciful forms, which overpower the naturalism of Peter Fuchs and the stylized foliage-work of which already seem to point toward Jugendstil (Art Nouveau), are even surpassed by the incredibly charming reliefs of the Wise 30, 31 and Foolish Virgins by Wilhelm Mengelberg on the portals on the north side.

30, 31   The medaillions with representation of the Wise and Foolish Virgins from the bronze doors, made 1891–1897, on the central portal of the north façade are among the best works by Wilhelm Mengelberg.

This versatile Cologne artist, who had moved his workshop to Utrecht during the cultural wars, also made the *Stations of the Cross,* mounted 1893–1897 along the walls in the nave. The 13th station, the Pl 79 Lamentation, was executed as a large monolithic sculpture with subtle polychromy in the ground floor of the south tower and roofed over by an elaborate Neo-Gothic canopy. For the reverse side of the Altarpiece of St. Clare, he painted a large-scale represen-Pl 78 tation of the Holy Trinity in glowing colors in 1905.

Pl 15, 61 The *mosaic floor* in the chevet became the largest Pl 74, 75 item of decoration of the 19th century. From 1885 on August Essenwein, who also conceived the theological-metamorphic program, drew the designs. When he died in 1892, merely his catalogue of bishops in the ambulatory and the crossing, presently covered over, were finished. Fritz Geiges continued the work until 1899, executing the panels in the east area of the inner choir following Essenwein's designs. The mosaics, made of multi-colored ceramic material, were manufactured by Villeroy & Boch in Mettlach. After it had been almost completely ignored by the public and by art history for almost one hundred years, there is presently a growing interest in this eccentric work, unique in its own way.

In 1873 entries were solicited for a public competi-Pl 70 tion for a complete Neo-Gothic renovation of the chevet, whereupon many interesting designs were submitted. Not only the expense involved hindered the execution, but probably more so indeed the inability to arrive at a consensus of opinion on such a difficult matter. Thus, after endless discussions during which the project was proving to become increasingly Pl 69 questionable, the *axial chapel* was the only one to be renovated in the sense of Neo-Gothic interior decoration between 1889 and 1907. Such well-known artists as Friedrich Stummel and Wilhelm Mengelberg were involved. Instead of the floor mosaic, which became the victim of archaeological excavations in 1947, a slab covering made in Mettlach from the then demolished Dominican Church in Düsseldorf was laid in 1975.

Erosion, War, and Restoration

After the Festival for the Construction of the Cathedral in 1880, there was still much work remaining to be done; nevertheless, this also soon waned and the cathedral workshop, which in its best times employed over 500 people, shrunk down to a small core. Yet only for a few years did the Cathedral remain really complete in all its parts, undamaged and without scaffolding. Already in 1904 when the damage on the buttress-

ing of the chevet could no longer be overlooked and parts built in the 19th century already even came tumbling down, Cathedral Architect Bernhard Hertel (1903–1927) began to increment the workshop again. He and his sucessor, Hans Güldenpfennig (1928–1944), renewed the entire buttressing of the chevet in Pl 5, 6 shell-limestone by 1940, which seen today was a serious mistake, because after only a few years this material already began to become severly damaged by weathering.

32   North transept after World War II

During World War II fourteen air-bombs hit the Cathedral, although one must assume that all war-making powers tried to spare this world-famous building. Ten vaults in the nave and north transept collapsed, all the window tracery was damaged, and the gable of the north façade tumbled down and buried the large organ under it. In the north pier buttress on the west façade a parachute mine tore a dangerously deep cavity, which had to be patched immediately with bricks. It remains in this state even today, reminding us of the horrors of war.

After the war Cathedral Architect Willy Weyres (1944–1972) was commissioned to make at least the chevet usable again by the anniversary year 1948, which he also achieved under indescribable toil. However, not until 1956 were the heavily damaged west parts also returned to church services.

Among the art works made at this time the *bronze portals of the south transept façade* by Ewald Mataré, installed between 1948 and 1954, deserve special attention. Willy Weyres personally created a number of *stained-glass windows* in order to close in the immense areas in the clerestory of the nave. He created particularly fanciful forms in the north side aisle of the chevet over the doors to the sacristy. In a later phase the sculptor Elmar Hillebrand worked for the Cathedral. He in particular is responsible for the cast-bronze works in the area of the crossing altar, erected in 1960. Paul Nagel contributed the powerful wrought-iron grills in the area of the crypt. Under the organ gallery, built by Weyres in 1948, Peter Hecker painted his last monumental work in 1964.

In 1962 the cathedral workshop began to restore the façade on the north transept, which was particularly severely devastated. These endeavors could not be finished until 1982, directed by Cathedral Architect Arnold Wolff (in office since 1972).

Nonetheless construction continues. As in the Middle Ages a cathedral workshop constantly accompanies the life of the Cathedral, the stone of which is being eaten away by wind and weather, and often even more so by air pollution. An operation with about 85 employees takes care that the ruined parts of the building are replaced in weatherproof material. The damage by war is also still far from being repaired. Not only the stonework needs its care, but also the roofs, the eaves troughs, and the roof enclosures have to be maintained. The stained-glass windows require particular attention, the maintenance of which is cared for by the largest glass restoration workshop in Europe. A special department concerns itself with the archaeology under the floor of the Cathedral, where evidence of the last two thousand years is yet to be excavated. Art historians care for the furnishings of

32
Pl 1

Pl 4, 87

Pl 68

33, 34
Pl 90–93

33 A stonemason of the cathedral workshop working on a Gothic workpiece

34 Stonemasons of the cathedral workshop mounting a renewed flying buttress

the interior, the many models of sculptures, and the vast archives of the Cathedral.

It can be predicted that the workshop, under certain circumstances later in a diminished form, must always remain in operation, and also constantly carry out projects on the exterior. No one living today will ever see the Cathedral without scaffolding. As a Cologne saying puts it: when the Cathedral is finished, the world will end.

Bibliography

Kölner Domblatt (abbreviated KDBl.): *Amtliche Mittheilungen des Central-Dombau-Vereins*, published weekly, No.1, 1842 to No. 132, 1844; published monthly, No. 1, 1844 to No. 331, 1892.

Kölner Domblatt: Jahrbuch des Zentral-Dombau-Vereins, No. 1, 1948 to No. 50, 1989 (is being continued).

Boisserée, Sulpiz. *Ansichten, Risse, und einzelne Theile des Doms von Köln.* Stuttgart, 1821–1832; 2nd ed. Munich, 1842; revised edition, ed. by Arnold Wolff, Cologne, 1979.

Schmitz, Franz. *Der Dom zu Köln. Seine Konstruktion und Ausstattung.* Cologne/Neuss, 1868–1879; 2nd ed., Frankfurt, 1910.

Ennen, Leonard. *Der Dom zu Köln von seinem Beginne bis zu seiner Vollendung. Festschrift.* Cologne, 1880.

Der Dom zu Köln. Volume published on the occasion of the 50th anniversary of its completion on October 15, 1880, ed. by Erich Kuphal, Cologne, 1930.

Clemen, Paul. *Der Dom zu Köln.* 2nd ed., Düsseldorf, 1938 *(Die Kunstdenkmäler der Rheinprovinz VI/3).*

Der Kölner Dom. Volume published on the occasion of the 700th anniversary, 1248–1948, ed. by the Friends of the Cathedral Society *(Zentral-Dombau-Verein).* Cologne, 1948.

Hoster, Joseph. *Der Dom zu Köln.* Cologne, 1965.

Wolff, Arnold. *Der Kölner Dom.* Stuttgart, 1974; 5th ed., 1988; english edition: *The Cathedral of Cologne.* Translated by Margret Maranuk-Rohmeder. Stuttgart, 1980; 3rd ed., 1989.

Rode, Herbert. *Die mittelalterlichen Glasmalereien des Kölner Domes (Corpus Vitrearum Medii Aevi).* Berlin, 1974.

Das Kölner Dom Jubiläumsbuch 1980. Official volume published by the High Cathedral of Cologne, ed. by Arnold Wolff and Toni Diederich. Cologne, 1980.

Der Kölner Dom im Jahrhundert seiner Vollendung. Catalogue and volume of essays, ed. by Hugo Borger. Cologne, 1980.

Borger, Hugo. *Der Dom zu Köln.* Cologne, 1980.

Doppelfeld, Otto and Willy Weyres. *Die Ausgrabungen im Dom zu Köln,* ed. by Hansgerd Hellenkemper. Mainz, 1980 *(Kölner Forschungen,* vol. 1).

Klein, Adolf. *Der Dom zu Köln. Die bewegte Geschichte seiner Vollendung.* Cologne, 1980.

Schulten, Walter. *Der Kölner Domschatz.* Cologne, 1980.

Wolff, Arnold. *Dombau in Köln. Photographen dokumentieren die Vollendung einer Kathedrale.* Stuttgart, 1980.

Religion – Kunst – Vaterland. Der Kölner Dom im 19. Jahrhundert, ed. by Otto Dann. Cologne, 1983.

Wolff, Arnold. *Vorbericht über die Ergebnisse der Kölner Domgrabung, 1946–1983.* Opladen, 1983 *(Forschungsberichte des Landes Nordrhein-Westfalen,* No. 3000).

Verschwundenes Inventarium. Der Skulpturenfund im Kölner Domchor. Exhibition catalogue. Cologne, 1984.

Weyres, Willy. *Die vorgotischen Bischofskirchen in Köln.* (*Studien zum Kölner Dom,* vol. 1). Cologne, 1987.

Photographic Sources

Fridmar Damm: Pl 3

Wim Cox: Pl 46

Dombauarchiv Cologne: Ill. 12, 31, 33; Pl 47–55, 77, 83–85, 92

Rainer Gaertner: Ill. 15, 18; Pl 1, 2, 4, 7–11, 22, 24–26, 29–31, 33, 59, 61, 64, 65, 67, 75, 79, 86, 87, 89, 94

Reiner Palm: Ill. 21

Rheinisches Bildarchiv, Cologne: Ill. 20–21, 25, 29–32; Pl 18, 20, 28, 70–74, 80–82; Helmut Buchen: Pl 6, 21, 27, 32, 38–45, 56, 60, 62, 63, 66, 76, 78; Wolfgang F. Meier: Pl 23, 34–37, 57, 58, 69

Verlag Kölner Dom: Ill. 1, 2, 11, 17

Arnold Wolff: Ill. 3–10, 13, 14, 16, 22–24, 28; Pl 5, 12–17, 19, 68, 88, 90, 91, 93

Legends for the Color Plates

Pl 1 The west façade of the Cathedral, 157 meters/515 feet high. Begun c. 1300, completed on October 15, 1880.

Pl 2 The west façade above the ground story.

Pl 3 View of the entire Cathedral from the south.

Pl 4 The south transept façade, designed and built by Cathedral Architect Ernst Friedrich Zwirner, 1842–1855.

Pl 5 The clerestory of the chevet from the south. Above the very simple ground story (c. 1250–1260), rise the richly organized flying buttresses supported by the slender pier buttresses between the large windows (c. 1270–1300).

Pl 6 The chevet from the east: chapels, begun in 1248; clerestory, completed c. 1300.

Pl 7 Panorama of the Rhine River bank in Cologne. The Cathedral impressively rises above the modern city, in which only a few buildings, like the towers of Gross St. Martin and the City Hall, remind us of its medieval size.

Pl 8 View from the choir into the nave, completed in 1863.

Pl 9 View from the west into the choir, consecrated in 1322.

Pl 10 The upper choir facing east with the Windows of the Kings, installed 1300–1310.

Pl 11 The vaults of the axial chapel and the ambulatory, completed c. 1265.

Pl 12 The vault of the first story of the south tower, completed in 1876. The walls and window tracery were made in the 14th century.

Pl 13 The ground story of the south tower. Walls and piers, early 14th century; vault, 1876.

Pl 14 The crossing. The vaults of the crossing, nave (below) and transept, 45 meters/147.5 feet high, were roofed over in 1863. Most of them collapsed in World War II and were renewed by 1956, recognizable by the historiated bosses (below and on the right). Above, the choir, completed c. 1300.

Pl 15 View from the inner part of the south ambulatory toward the west. Piers and vaults, completed c. 1265; choir stalls, before 1322; mosaic floor, c. 1890. In the background is the south side of the nave; piers, 14th century; vault, 1842–1848.

Pl 16 The north wall of the nave toward the west. The piers and the last three arches were constructed in the 15th and early 16th centuries; the rest of the parts, 1842–1863.

Pl 17 The north wall of the choir, seen from the south part of the ambulatory. All architectural parts, 1248–1300; the Windows of the Kings, 1300–1310; the angels in the spandrels of the arcades in the ground story, by Edward von Steinle, 1843–1846. The glazing of the triforium, 19th and 20th centuries.

Pl 18 A flying buttress for the chevet, built c. 1270–1290. Drawing by Kronenberg, 1823–1825; pencil, ink, and watercolor on cardboard, 273 × 142 cm/c. 106.5 × 55.5 in. Cologne, Dombau-archiv.

Pl 19 The buttressing over the south side of the nave, built 1855–1863 using the chevet as a model. In the background, the south tower:

below, 14th century; from the middle of the picture upwards, 1869–1875.

Pl 20 The unfinished Cathedral in its environs, condition c. 1780. Painted plaster of Paris model in a scale of 1:200; built by Hans Boffin using measurements by Ludwig Arntz, c. 1925. View from the northwest. The model quite accurately shows the state of construction. The crossing was also covered by roofs, not open as shown here. However, the Romanesque bishop's palace in the background, built under Archbishop Reinald von Dassel (1159–1167), no longer existed for some time.

Pl 21 St. Catherine. One of the 34 archivolt statues from the Portal of St. Peter (Pl 22); light-colored limestone, height 67 cm/c. 26 in., carved c. 1375 by sculptors from the School of the Parlers.

Pl 22 The Portal of St. Peter. This portal, 11 meters / 36 feet high up to the point of the arch, is the only one of the nine portals to be completed in the Middle Ages. The sculptural decoration was carved by sculptors of the School of the Parlers, c. 1375; the darker statues in the foreground, by Peter Fuchs, 1880. The bronze door, 1889, was designed by Hugo Schneider. The lintel (darker areas), destroyed in the war, was reconstructed by Serban Rusu and Giuseppe Lotito in 1979.

Pl 23 The pastoral staff of St. Peter (upper part). The ivory head is possibly still Roman; the metal parts date from various centuries. They cover the actual relics of the staff.

Pl 24 The Hillinus Codex, dedication illumination. Hillinus, a priest of the Cathedral, gives the book which he had made at his own expense to St. Peter. Above this scene the upper part of a church building can be seen, which is interpreted as the Old Cathedral. Manuscript with miniatures, c. 1025; size of a leaf, 37 × 27 cm/ c. 14.5 × 10.5 in.; Cod. Metr. Col. 12. Cologne, Dombibliothek.

Pl 25 Grave Slab of Archbishop Gero (969–976) in the Chapel of St. Stephen, white marble, red porphyry, and Lacedaemonian (green) porphyry inlaid on a slab of red sandstone. Pictured is only the panel of inlay, c. 197 × 50 cm/c. 77 × 19.5 in.

Pl 26 The Gero Crucifix, commissioned by Archbishop Gero, before 976. Corpus (1.87 meters/c. 6 feet high) and cross (2.85 meters/c. 9 feet high), oak. Polychromy, painted over numerous times; the last time, c. 1900.

Pl 27 The translation of the relics of the Three Magi to Milan and Cologne. Scenes from the cycle of pictures on the choir screen paintings in the Cathedral of Cologne, 14th century.

Pl 28 Water-colored drawing, 1633. In front of the iron gate, painted red, a pew and to the left of it a poor-box can be seen. To the right in front of the grating of the Chapel of St. Irmgard, lies the part of a turret which fell through the vaulting-cell of the axial chapel on October 7, 1434, and barely missed hitting the shrine. The hole made in the vault was indicated by an inscription. Cologne, Kölnisches Stadtmuseum.

Pl 29 The front of the Shrine of the Three Magi. In the lower area, the Adoration of the Three Magi (l.) and the Baptism of Christ (r.). In the middle the Virgin is enthroned with the Christ Child. Above the removable trapezoid-shaped plate in the upper pediment of the gable is a representation of the Second Coming of Christ at the Last Judgement.

Pl 30 View of the entire shrine after restoration by Fritz Zehgruber and Peter Bolg, 1961–1973.

Pl 31 The prophet Jonah from the David-side of the shrine after restoration by Fritz Zehgruber and Peter Bolg.

Pl 32 Representation of the Virgin Enthroned with the Christ Child and the Adoration of the Three Magi, with Otto IV (1198–1215) in their entourage. The front of the Shrine of the Three Magi.

Pl 33 View to the south side of the inner choir with the choir stalls and the choir screen paintings. The choir screen scenes represented here show the end of the Legend of the Three Magi with their consecration as bishops by St. Thomas, their funeral, then first the translation of their remains to Constantinople with St. Helen, then to Milan, and finally to Cologne.

Pl 34–37 Grotesques on the choir stalls.

Pl 38–42 Details of the choir screen paintings from the band of writing under the scenes of the legends.

Pl 43 Detail from the Life of the Virgin on the south side of the choir screens with the Nativity of the Virgin and the Annunciation.

Pl 44 The high altar, detail: the Coronation of the Virgin with Sts. John the Evangelist and Peter, the patron of the altar.

Pl 45 Three of the fourteen pillar statues in the choir: Christ, Sts. Peter and Andrew, radiating in the richness of their patterned garments, on consoles with different foliage-work, under canopies in two variations.

Pl 46 Virgin Mary, from the series of pillar statues in the choir.

Pl 47 One of the 48 kings from the clerestory in the choir.

Pl 48 Virgin Mary, detail from the scene of the Nativity from the »Younger Biblical Window« in the Chapel of St. Stephen, formerly in the choir of the Dominican Church of the Holy Cross, c. 1280.

Pl 49–52 The Sacrifice of Isaac and the Crucifixion of Christ, the Feast of Abraham and the Last Supper, scenes from the »Elder Biblical Window«, c. 1260, made as the central window for the axial chapel in the Cathedral.

Pl 53 The Window of the Three Magi in the axial chapel.

Pl 54 A panel of ornamental design over the Window of the Three Magi in the axial chapel.

Pl 55 The Cologne hero Marsilius, a detail from the Window of the Nativity in the north side aisle. The bill was paid by the Cologne City Council on March 29, 1508.

Pl 56 The Window of the Nativity, completed in 1508, in the north side aisle with two coats of arms of the City of Cologne, accompanied by Agrippa and Marsilius in the lower level. Above this from left to right, Sts. George, Mauritius, Gereon, and Albinus. In the next series of pictures, the Nativity and on the left – as a typological prefiguration in the Old Testament – Moses before the burning thorn bush.

Pl 57 Duke Gottfried von Arnsberg († 1372), a detail of his effigy in the western part of the Chapel of Our Lady.

Pl 58 Grave monument for Archbishop Philipp von Heinsberg († 1191), during whose reign the construction of the large city wall was begun, made c. 1300, with a representation of the city wall and the oldest existing coat of arms of the city of Cologne.

Pl 59 St. Christopher, Master Tilman, the last quarter of the 15th century.

Pl 60 On the pillar across from the Statue of St. Christopher stands the elegant »Beautiful Madonna« from c. 1400.

Pl 61 View into the choir. Architecture and furnishings (with the exception of the floor and the spandrels in the arcades), completed in the early 14th century.

Pl 62 Altarpiece of St. Clare, detail: the Flight to Egypt (c. 1350).

Pl 63 Altarpiece of St. Clare, detail: the Annunciation to the Shepherds (c. 1400).

Pl 64 Stephan Lochner, Altarpiece of the City Patrons, detail: the Companions of St. Gereon.

Pl 65 The folding picture reproduces the Altarpiece of the City Patrons in its entirety, which Stephan Lochner made c. 1445 for the Chapel of the City Council. Opened it measures 5.22 meters/17 feet wide × 2.82 meters/9 feet high. Not until 1809 did this triptych enter the Cathedral.

Pl 66 Detail of the Altarpiece of the Three Magi in the Chapel of St. Maternus. This altarpiece, made in Antwerp in the first quarter of the 16th century, came into the possession of the Cathedral as an exchange in 1960.

Pl 67 The middle section of the Altarpiece of St. Agilolphus, 6.8 meters/22 feet wide and 5.5 meters/18 feet high, made in Antwerp in 1521 and located in the south transept, shows scenes from the Public Ministry of Christ and his Passion. The large statue of a bishop with a sword over the right wing represents the martyr Agilolphus; on the left is Archbishop Anno II (1056–1075) with a model of a church. It indicates him as the founder of the collegiate church, St. Mary *ad gradus* (at the stairs) situated to the east of the Cathedral, from which the altarpiece came into the Cathedral after the secularization.

Pl 68 The north wall of the nave, seen from the south side aisle. The piers date from the 14th and 15th centuries; the two western arches (l.) including the triforium ledge, 16th century; the other parts, 1842–1863. The windows are by Willy Weyres, 1950–1956.

Pl 69 The axial chapel, already finished in the vertex of the ambulatory in 1261, was decorated by Friedrich Stummel with Neo-Gothic wall paintings integrating remnants of medieval frescoes in 1891. Wilhelm Mengelberg made the altarpiece as well as the statues of the Three Magi in 1908; the so-called »Madonna from Füssenich«, donated by Alexander Schnütgen, dates from the 13th century. In 1978 the axial chapel (the Chapel of the Three Magi) was restored.

Pl 70 In connection with a competition which took place in 1873 for the decoration of the interior of the Cathedral, August Rincklake drew this design of a superstructure on the high altar, in which the Shrine of the Three Magi is also integrated. Presently in the Dombauarchiv.

Pl 71 Detail from the third of a series of tapestries, designed by Johann Anton Ramboux with representations of the Nicene Creed, which were embroidered between 1851 and 1857 by a Cologne women's club and hung in front of the choir screen paintings until 1920. Presently in the Cologne Seminary of the Archbishop for Priests.

Pl 72 The first of a series of eight tapestries, which were woven following cartoons by Peter Paul Rubens, c. 1640, and donated to the Cathedral in 1688, shows the Meeting of Abraham and Melchizedek.

Pl 73 This oil painting, painted by the Nazarene Friedrich Overbeck between 1847 and 1855, which served as an altarpiece on the

Altar of Our Lady until the end of World War II and presently hangs in the south transept, combines the Assumption of the Virgin with motives from representations of the Immaculate Conception.

Pl 74 Following the »Revised General Design for the Flooring of the Cathedral« by August Essenwein from 1887, the mosaic floor was laid until 1899. Presently in the Dombauarchiv.

Pl 75 The mosaic panel in the vertex of the ambulatory shows Archbishop and Electoral Prince Konrad von Hochstaden with the plan of the Gothic Cathedral, for which he laid the foundation stone in 1248. A monk with a staff and mitre and a knight with a sword, a shield, and a helmet indicate the religious and worldy power of the archbishop.

Pl 76 The central »Bavarian Window« in the south aisle, commissioned by King Ludwig I of Bavaria, manufactured in the Royal Manufactory for Stained Glass in Munich, 1842–1848, shows the Lamentation in the main panel and the Last Supper in the center above it; in the pinnacles, the »*Noli me tangere*« and the »Incredulity of Thomas«; in the base arcades, the Four Evangelists.

Pl 77 The window in the south transept, designed by Georg Fortner and Heinrich Ainmiller, executed by Leonhard Faustner in Munich in 1855/56, shows Joseph Görres, who called for the completion of the Cathedral in the *Rheinische Merkur* in 1814, in the stance of a medieval patron accompanied by his patron saint and kneeling in front of the Virgin and Child.

Pl 78 In order to cover up the unfinished reverse side of the Altarpiece of St. Clare after it was erected behind the high altar, Wilhelm Mengelberg painted at the suggestion of Alexander Schnütgen this large-scale representation of the »Seat of Mercy« in Neo-Gothic style in 1905.

Pl 79 In the entrance hall under the south tower, a sculptural group of the Lamentation under an architectonic canopy closes the cycle of the Stations of the Cross, carved by Wilhelm Mengelberg between 1893 and 1897.

Pl 80 The construction of the portals on the south transept. Behind the new piers appear the provisional separating walls of the transept from around 1265 (r.) and 1388 (l. with Gothic-arched windows); on the far right, the cathedral workshop. Water-colored pencil drawing by Johann Anton Ramboux, February, 1844, 107 × 60 cm/c. 41.5 × 23.5 in., Cologne, Kölnisches Stadtmuseum.

Pl 81 Construction of the north transept façade. Behind the provisional separating wall of the 13th and 14th centuries, the sacristy is on the left with the north building, which was razed in 1866. To the far right, the south tower with the crane. Water-colored pencil drawing by Johann Anton Ramboux, June–July, 1845; 103.5 × 83.7 cm/c. 40.5 × 32.5 in., Cologne, Kölnisches Stadtmuseum.

Pl 82 The Festival for Construction of the Cathedral on October 3, 1855. In no other picture are the supporters of continued construction so close together: the Prussian House of Kings, the Friends of the Cathedral Society *(Zentral-Dombau-Verein = ZDV)*, and the laborers. To the left on a raised platform, King Friedrich IV accompanied by Prince Wilhelm and Archbishop Johannes von Geissel with Suffragon Baudri and other canons of the Cathedral. In the center, the Friends of the Cathedral Society *(Zentral-Dombau-Verein)*: in the front, Mayor Strupp and the president of the ZDV, the Counselor of Justice Ferdinand Esser; to the left of them, Heinrich von Wittgenstein; to the

right, August Reichensperger and his friend von Thimus. Behind the workmen stands Cathedral Architect Zwirner. The finial in front of him was designated for the north portal and »for comparison of size [...] placed here at the foot of the south portal«. Water-colored pencil drawing, 53.5 × 67 cm/c. 21 × 26 in., second design by Edward von Steinle for the scene in the cycle of pictures, »The Completion of the Cathedral«, in the staircase of the former Wallraf-Richartz-Museum, executed in 1863. Cologne, Kölnisches Stadtmuseum.

Pl 83 The Cathedral from the southeast. Photo by Johann Franz Michiels, late 1855, taken from the tower of Gross St. Martin, 43 × 54 cm/c. 17 × 21 in., Cologne, Dombauarchiv.

Pl 84 The beginning of continued construction on the west façade. Photo by Ch. Marville, late summer, 1853, 35.3 × 25.6 cm/c. 14 × 10 in., Cologne, Dombauarchiv.

Pl 85 The Cathedral from the east after October 15, 1880. Photo by Anselm Schmitz, 50.8 × 40 cm/c. 20 × 15.5 in., Cologne, Dombauarchiv.

Pl 86 Christian Mohr carried out the entire sculptural decoration of the south transept façade following drawings by Ludwig Schwanthaler between 1849 and 1871, among others, also these statues of the martyrs Stephen, Agnes, Apolinaris, and Pantaleon on the right jamb of the central portal.

Pl 87 The bronze doors by Hugo Schneider, installed in 1891, destroyed in World War II, were replaced by the doors on the south portal by Ewald Mataré, made between 1948 and 1954, the bronze reliefs of which are accentuated by mosaics on certain parts – i. e., the representation of the pelican as a symbol of love on the right door of the central portal, dedicated to Pope Pius XII.

Pl 88 Between 1834 and 1841 the Cologne sculptor Wilhelm Joseph Imhoff created twelve music-making angels following drawings by Karl Friedrich Schinkel for the so-called »Little Houses of the Saints«, the canopies on the pier buttresses of the chevet. Presently in the lapidarium of the Cathedral.

Pl 89 All the sculptures on the central portal of the west façade were carved by Peter Fuchs between 1872 and 1880: on the trumeau, Virgin Mary, Mother of Christ; on the jambs, the predecessors of Christ; in the tympanum, scenes and in the archivolts statues from the Old Testament. Nine angels with tools of torture on the slopes of the gable, by Erlefried Hoppe, 1955/56. The bronze doors were designed by Hugo Schneider and mounted in 1887.

Pl 90 The buttressing system on the north side of the nave. Just as on the medieval chevet, it is simpler in its arrangement than that of the south side (Pl 19). Readily visible is the severe damage due to weathering on the sandstone from Schlaitdorf.

Pl 91 The gable and gallery on the northwest corner of the north transept. Except for the tracery in the windows and their foliated frames, all the parts were completely renewed in basalt lava from Londorf by the cathedral workshop in 1982.

Pl 92 An angel for the gable of the Portal of St. Peter, c. 1.9 meters/c. 6 feet high, limestone from Savonnières, Peter Fuchs, 1880. Photographed by Anselm Schmitz shortly before being mounted.

Pl 93 The same angel in 1985. The severe damage by weathering, the crust of dirt and the growth of algae are encouraged by the present air pollution.

Pl 94 The belfry in the second story of the southwest tower. In the center, the bell of St. Peter from 1923.

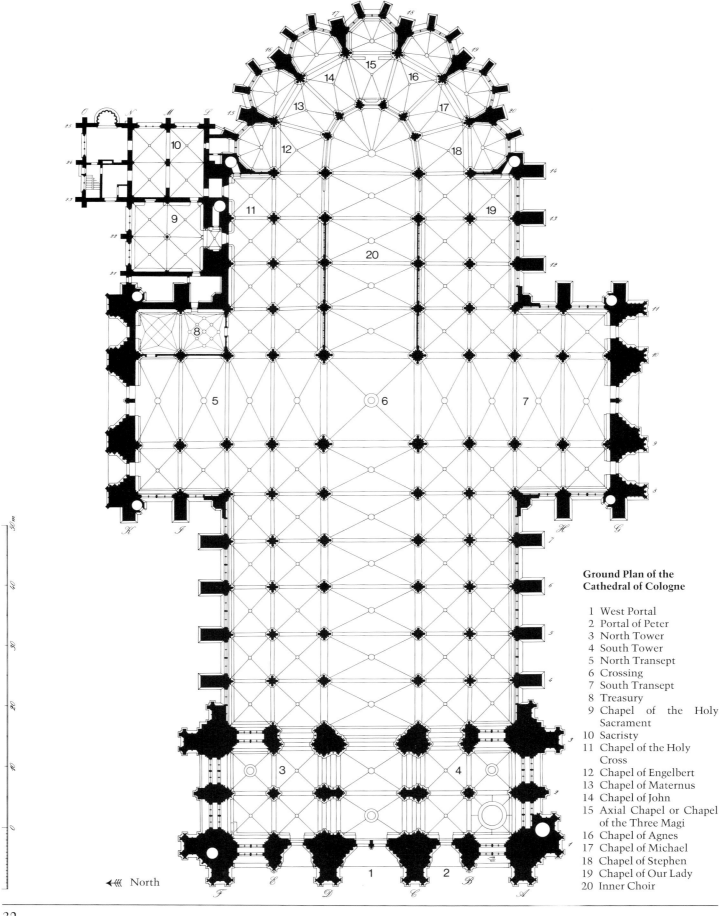

Ground Plan of the Cathedral of Cologne

1 West Portal
2 Portal of Peter
3 North Tower
4 South Tower
5 North Transept
6 Crossing
7 South Transept
8 Treasury
9 Chapel of the Holy Sacrament
10 Sacristy
11 Chapel of the Holy Cross
12 Chapel of Engelbert
13 Chapel of Maternus
14 Chapel of John
15 Axial Chapel or Chapel of the Three Magi
16 Chapel of Agnes
17 Chapel of Michael
18 Chapel of Stephen
19 Chapel of Our Lady
20 Inner Choir

◄⧏⧏ North

1

2 ▷

3   4

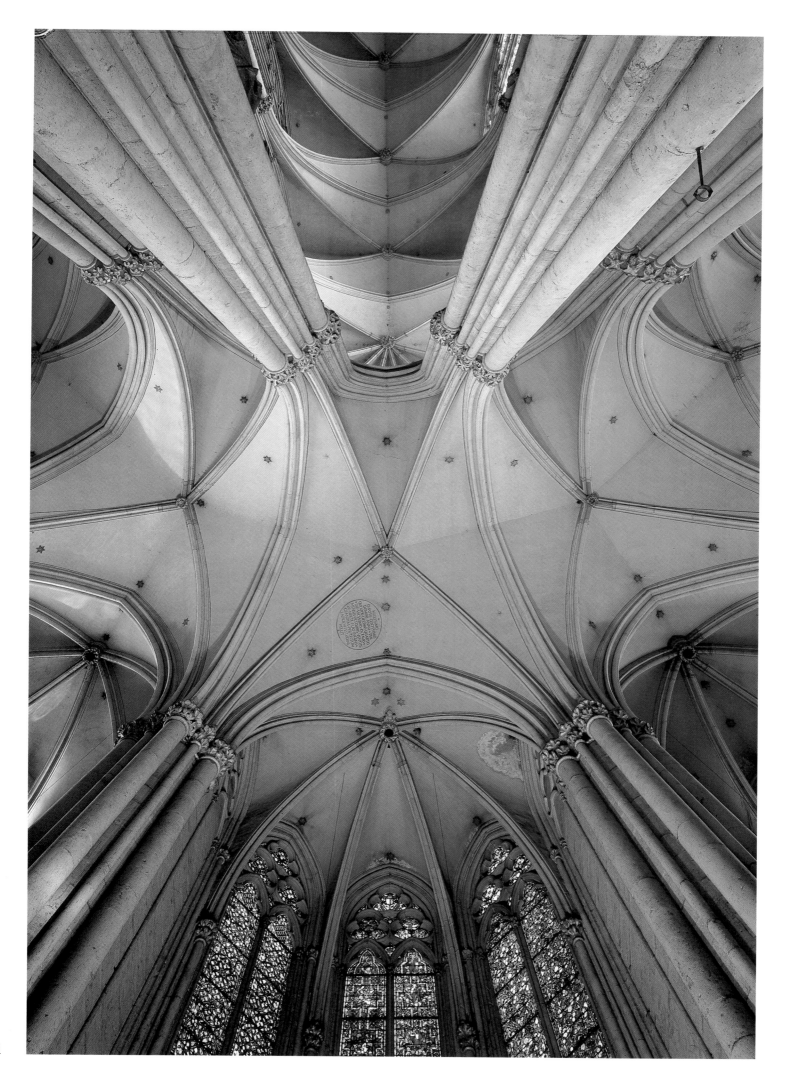

12

13

Westliche Ansicht der 1/2 Strebewand an der südlichen Seite des Chors

21

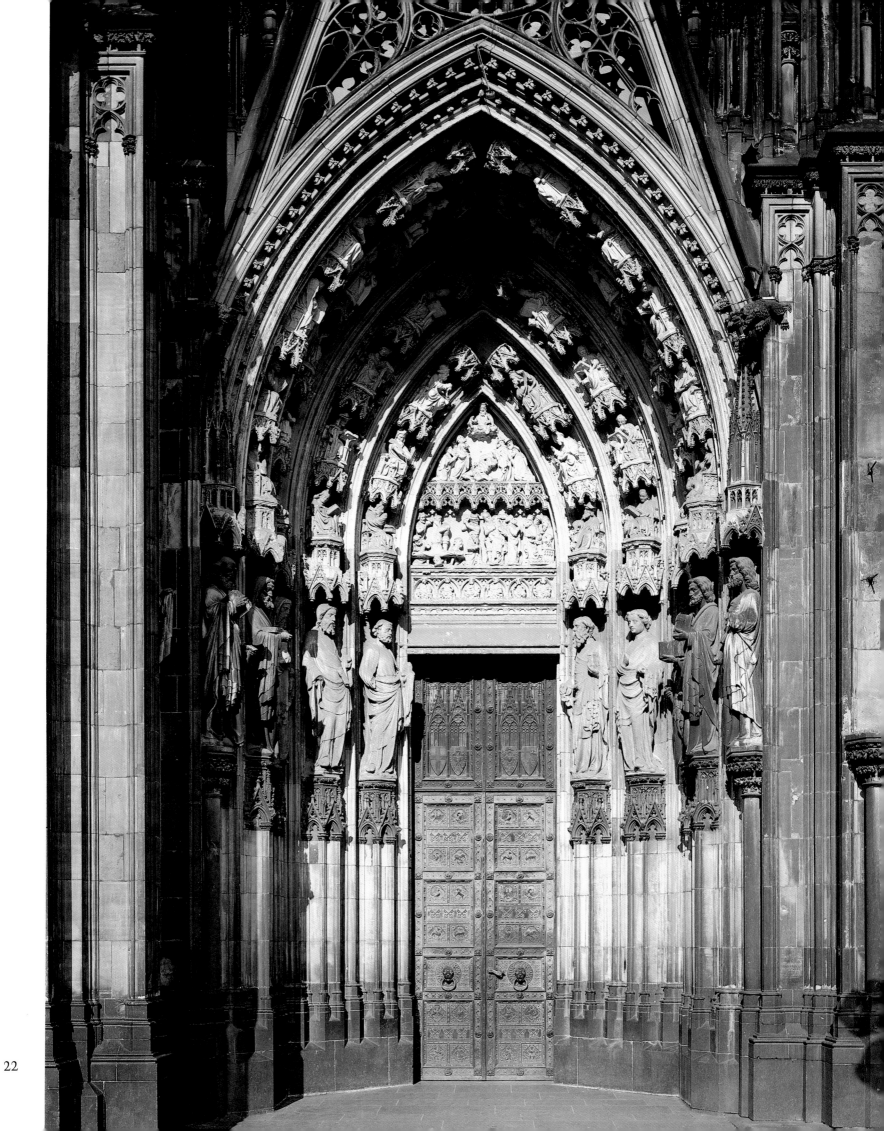

23

24 ▷

25 ▷ ▷

26 ▷ ▷

27

28

29 ▷

30

31 ▷

32 ▷

PROPTER · ME · OPTA · ECH
TEMPESTAS · MITTIT · MEONMARE

34

35

36

37

◁ 33

38

39

40

41

42

49

50

51

52

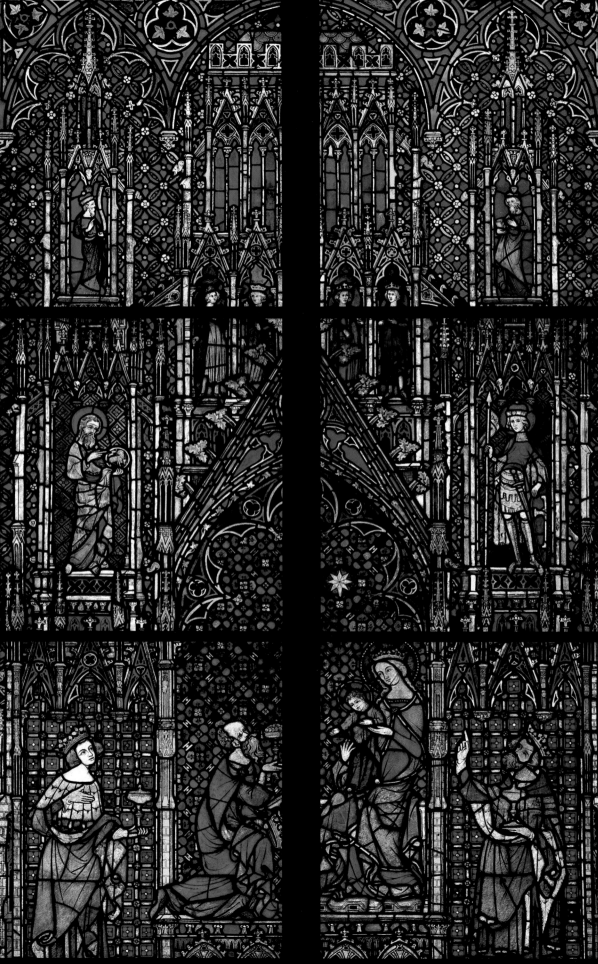

53

62

63

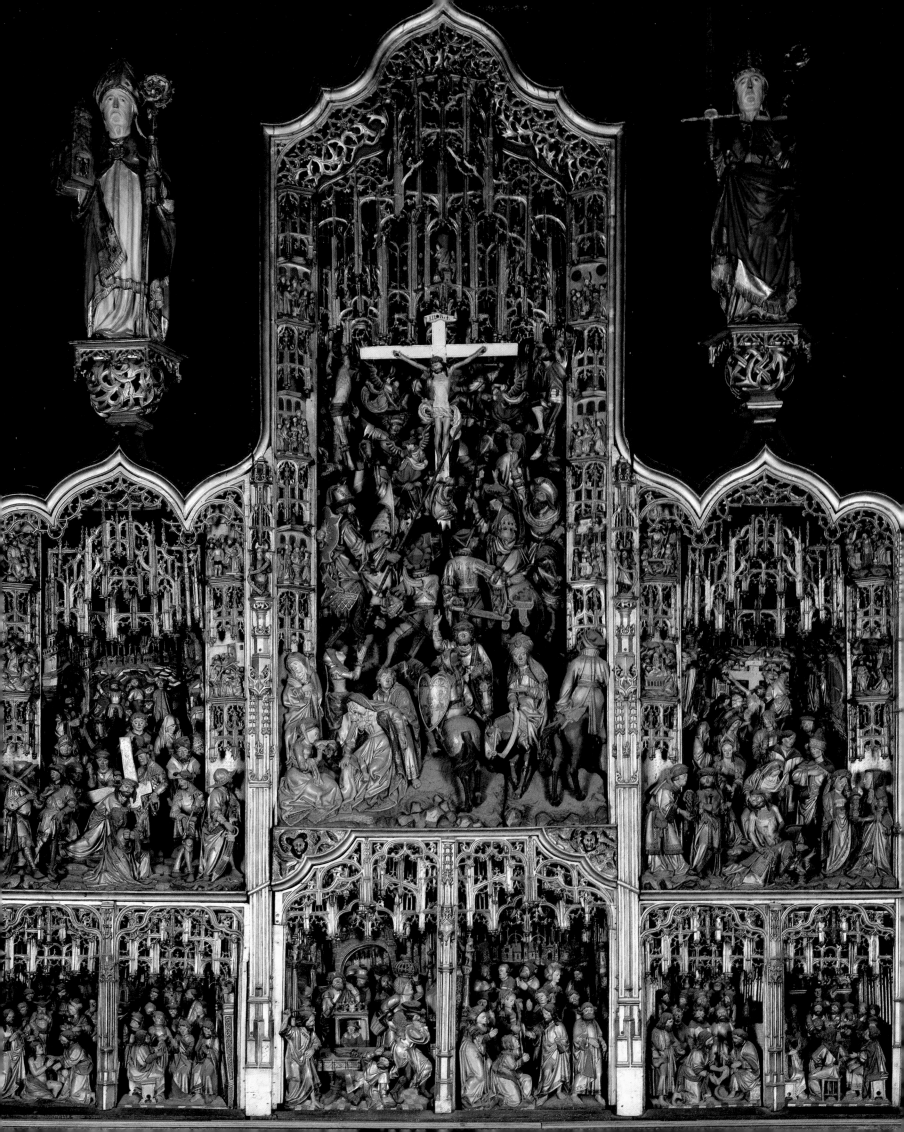

69

70

71

72

73

78

80

81

83

86

87

88

89 ▷

90

91

92

93 ▷

94